High Peak Drifter

ALSO BY
RICHARD BELL

Rough Patch
a sketchbook from the
wilder side of the garden
(Willow Island Editions)

Yorkshire Rock
a journey through time
(British Geological Survey)

Village Walks in
West Yorkshire
(Countryside Books)

High Peak Drifter

Richard Bell

Willow Island Editions

Willow Island Editions
ISBN 1-902467-16-7
© Richard Bell, 2006
www.willowisland.co.uk
41 Water Lane, Middlestown
Wakefield, West Yorkshire
WF4 4PX

Contents

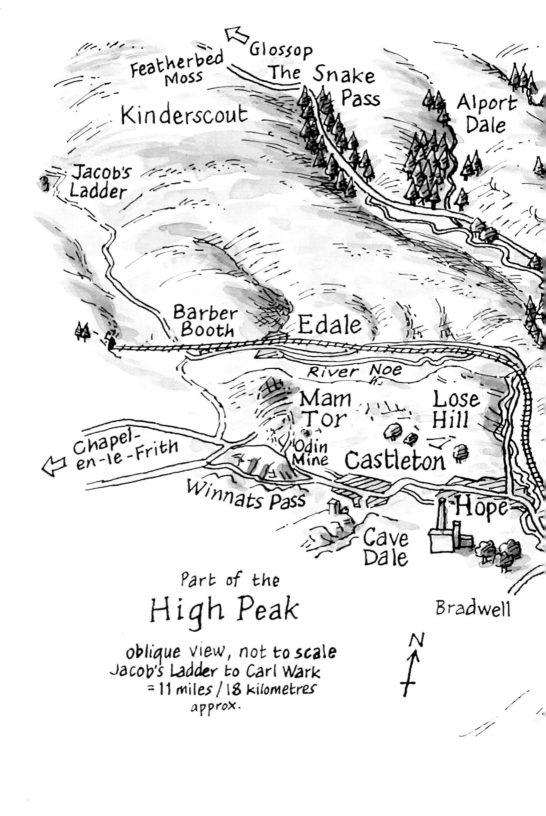

Glossop

Featherbed
Moss

The Snake
Pass

Alport
Dale

Kinderscout

Jacob's
Ladder

Barber
Booth

Edale

River Noe

Mam
Tor

Lose
Hill

Chapel-
en-le-Frith

Odin
Mine

Castleton

Winnats Pass

Cave
Dale

Hope

Part of the
High Peak

Bradwell

oblique view, not to scale
Jacob's Ladder to Carl Wark
= 11 miles / 18 kilometres
approx.

N

Howden
Reservoir

Derwent
Reservoir

Fairholmes

Derwent
Moors

Ladybower
Reservoir

Penistone

The Strines

Sheffield

Parkin Clough

Heatherdene

Win
Hill

Yorkshire
Bridge

Stanage Edge

Bamford

Hurst Clough

Hollin
Bank

Shatton

Hood Brook

Shatton Moor

River Derwent

Higger
Tor

Hathersage

Carl
Wark

The Snake

You'd hardly think that you could fit so much open space between Sheffield & Manchester.

Heather, peaty soil & gritstone fragments on the moor below the summit of Win Hill.

As I settle down in a cleft on the north side of the summit crag of Win Hill to draw the view towards the Snake Pass, the shadow of a tousled head appears over my sketchbook and I become aware of a gentle movement just behind me. Guessing that some hiker is taking an interest in my work, I turn and find myself looking right into the eyes of a black-faced sheep.

I say hello, expecting the sheep to baa in surprise and alarm and go running off but she just takes a cursory glance at my drawing and goes on nibbling. She soon turns around and I find myself eye to udder with her!

Pi! Pit!

Parachuting hang-gliding meadow pipit

9

I'm feeling restless this afternoon and I stride out along the ridge. The ridge is called a brink here: Thornhill Brink overlooks the Hope Valley, then, as the track swings around to the north-west, Hope Brink gives you views of the bulk of Lose Hill opposite then the Vale of Edale to the west.

I take a forest path down through the plantations of Woodland Valley to the top end of this arm of Ladybower Reservoir then follow the waterside track back to Heatherdene.

So why, when we've got ourselves out here to enjoy being in the Peak District, do we always want to be in some place else?

From the bench on the s. side of

Blue Circle
cement works
& quarry from
Win Hill.

Why this urge to go up hill, down dale
to see what's on the other side?

We get kitted up to march over moors,
tramp along trails and ride along the
ridges on mountain bikes.

All this activity is good for you,
but I think we also need time
just to drift; to stop for a
while and centre our-
selves on one small
patch of the planet.

Ladybower

Sandstone
outcrop near
Hathersage.

Spectacular scenery and mellow villages are what draw visitors to the Peak District but the experience of being here goes deeper than picture postcard prettiness; all the time you're here you're surrounded by 1001 small details; waterfalls, walls and gate-posts, things you might not even consciously notice; ferns, lichens and tree stumps... rocks, water, the changing sky.

To me they all seem connected, all part of the history of the Peak, and somehow I feel that there's a way in which we are all connected to them.

In our daily lives we're surrounded by ingeniously designed objects, glossy entertainments and up-to-the-minute bite-sized chunks of what's going on in the 'real' world. Someone has kindly thought it all out for us, so we can just grab what we need and get on with the busy-ness of our lives.

To me drawing is what brings me back down to earth . . .

. . . and so does just being here.

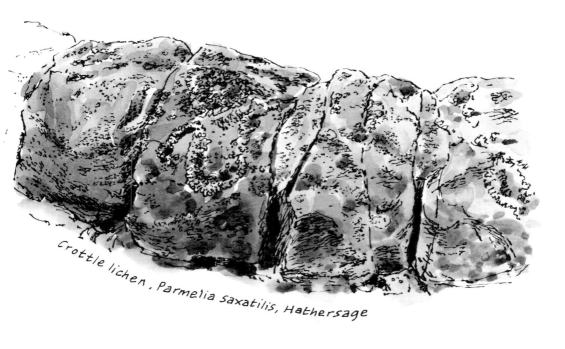

Crottle lichen, Parmelia saxatilis, Hathersage

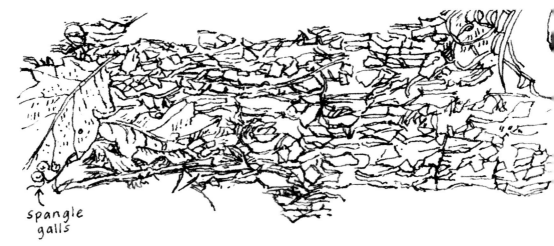

spangle
galls

Shale at Shatton

There's the White Peak – that's the limestone –
and the Dark Peak of Millstone Grit but, of
equal importance to the Peak landscape, there
are the shales in between. We tend to forget
about them because they don't form obvious
landmarks like crags and caves but it's
shale that accounts for the broad green
valleys. Being so soft it is soon cloaked
by soil except for the odd place like this
path climbing up from the River Noe at
Shatton where there's a small bank of
it that has been protected by some
old tree roots.

Shatton Moor from
the welcome shelter
of the Bay Tree Café
at the High Peak
Garden Centre.

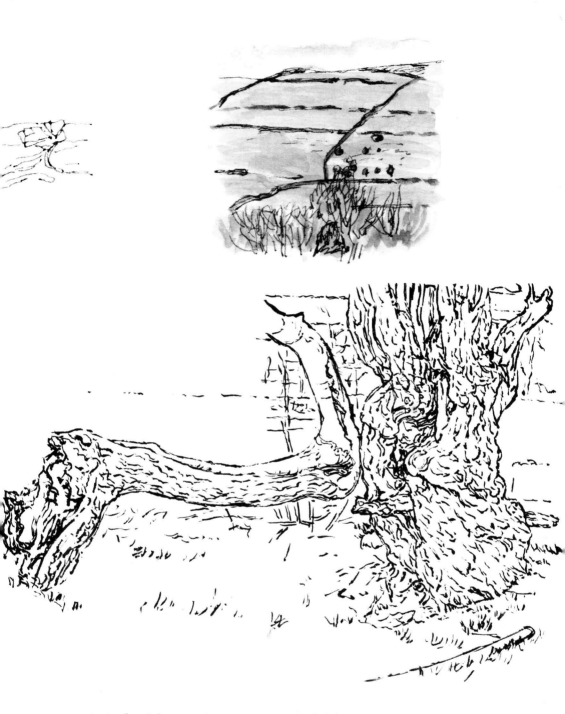

Ash & elder; cloud on the hill-tops
6°C but the wind from the NNE makes
it feel draughty on this hillside.

15

16

3pm from the edge of Shatton Moor,
looking over Bamford towards Ladybower.
Wind buffets the car and I'm hoping
there will be no problems with the hand-
brake on this hill.

Derwent Moors, beyond Ladybower
reservoir soon dissolve into mist as it
starts raining. I blot them out of my
drawing to try and get the same effect.

11.30 AM   25/10/05
Rush of brown water, frothy
rippling. Rattle of rain on my
fishing umbrella.

Why limit drawing in the Pea
If I keep things simple,
almost any weather: sketc
(to blot the ink to mak
a folding chair..

'Ford
Unsuitable for motors' says the
sign but this is where those big
4x4s they use for the school run
come into their own.

...District to warm sunny days?
...hould be able to work in
...ook, pen, waterbrush
...a makeshift wash)
...nd a fishing umbrella.

As repeated ripples hit the corner
of the culvert, the water pulses
and bubbles like an irregular
heartbeat.
A robin sings wistfully
in the rain.

Tchip!
Tchip!

A pair of dippers bob &
probe along the rivulets
running down the road.

Knobbly rhizomes of butterbur grow over mossy rocks at the edge of the River Noe and on the cement bags that protect the bridge.

River Noe, Shatton
1 pm 31/1/06

It seems that wherever you stop and look in the
Peak District there are more details — of history,
geology and natural history. Things that you'd
miss if you just kept on walking.

Thorn bush
Bamford 30/1/06
5°c looking N.

Further along this old hedge line
I drew a broken stone stile . . .
   my field notes are overleaf →

mole hills

weeds
meadow
grass?
+ bright
yell.green
tipped moss
on fallen
stone

Broken stone squeeze style.
former path, now apparently
Polished - by walkers or st
north side of post near to
marked post cattle use fie
post. 5°°: 4pm 30/1/06

12 thorns

TOP

Black feathers on top of post — sparrowhawk perch.

cow dung & yellow green granulated crust lichen on post

CLAYEY

WISPY

Remains of fox dropping at foot of post.

Claw marks dog? Fox? badger?

ght banking marks line of
ncated by railway.
? Bright green algae on
nd — dampness or dog
may scratch against

man-made history
rveyor told me: draughtsmans Chinese
watercolour sticks W+Newton.

OLD APPLE

(GOING BY THE LOOK OF ITS BRANCHES)

This old half-rotten tree serves as a corner post for a fence on Shatton Lane.

A robin sings from thorns across the lane.

Bright green moss grows as a thin shaggy carpet on the lower boughs.

There are a few patches of greyish lichen above, splodges of pale green below.

28 woodpecker holes?

Edale

Looking
towards
Edale Head
(hidden
by cloud)

A January morning: there's misty cloud and fine drizzle
over the Dark Peak so I head for the National Park
Centre at Edale to draw in the dry, warm shelter
of their displays. It is closed for re-building so I
set off along the back road to Mam Tor.

Most of the places that you can pull up are in
front of gates so when I see a lay-by that
doesn't seem to double as a passing place, I
pull up. Taking this random viewpoint, I
decide to spend the day drawing whatever
I can see around me.

The low cloud hangs in the Vale of Edale but clears as I draw Upper Holt Farm.

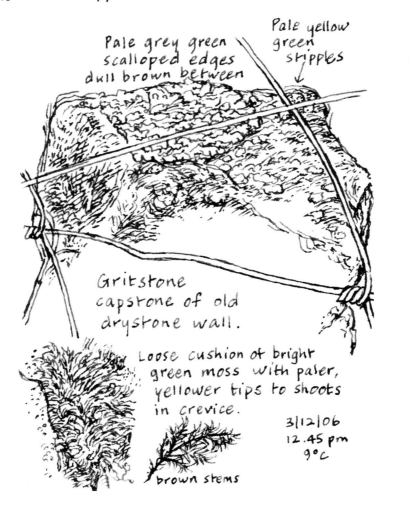

Pale grey green scalloped edges dull brown between

Pale yellow green stipples

Gritstone capstone of old drystone wall.

Loose cushion of bright green moss with paler, yellower tips to shoots in crevice.

3/12/06
12.45 pm
9°C

brown stems

There's a spot between these thorns
where sheep like to shelter.
After four hours drawing at this
little lay-by I'm chilled right
through, even though I've taken
breaks, sheltering in the car, for
flasks of hot drinks & sandwiches
but, like anywhere else in the
Peak District, there's so much
more I could have drawn here.

Autumn Journey

'Hello! Do you know where you're going? Because this doesn't lead anywhere.'

Last autumn I decided that the best way to get to know the Peak District was to walk right across it, from Sheffield to New Mills. Three minutes out of the station, confused by builders' fences, I'd already drifted into a concrete canyon behind the university. Lost already!

Thanks to the railway, I was able to break my trek into three stages, stopping at Hope and Edale.

Mam Tor from Edale
Station 4.15pm 14/11/05

Sheffield

30/1/06
11.30 am

Ladybower from
Heatherdene

Ladybower

Looking N.N.W. 8°C 100% cloud

Oak, beech, pine and birch grow at Heatherdene by Ladybower Dam. A robin sings a short melancholy trill against the intermittent roar of traffic on the Bamford road.

After getting chilled to the bone at Edale, I start the day by walking across the dam and back again to warm up.

A Scottish couple ask me if they could walk right around the reservoir : I guess they can but I later discover that this arm of the reservoir curves away further than you might think it does, making it a six mile round trip, returning along-side the busy A57 Snake Road.

Hope they made it!

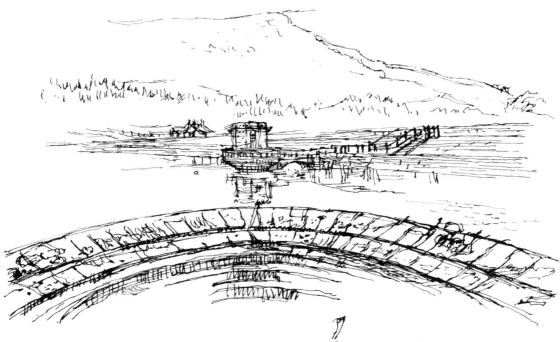

It's so spectacular, but this overflow proved too regular and mechanical as a subject. I haven't come to the Peak District to draw civil engineering, however impressive.

When I came back at the beginning of April – at a time when hose-pipe bans were in the offing in the south-east of England – the reservoir was full to overflowing and I couldn't resist taking a photograph.

But I still didn't want to draw it.

River Derwent
Yorkshire Bridge,
Ladybower

Beneath the spattering and rushing there's an undercurrent like a drum roll, like an avalanche about to start or a train about to enter the valley. Just as I'm thinking of the best way I might describe this, a large prop-driven RAF transport goes over. It is so low in the valley here that I guess it must have passed very low over the dam in a Dambusters style fly-by.

35

I like the expression of energy in the
rushing water and the way that contrasts
with the sombre solidity of the rocks —
irresistible force, immovable object.
And, unlike the overflow, it's <u>all</u> organic.

It's great to have the excuse to look closely
at something so natural for a few hours and
to be surrounded by the damp, mossy woodland

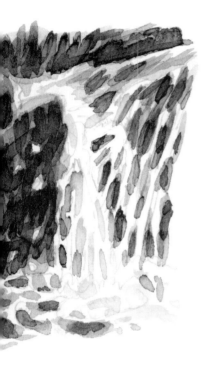

atmosphere of the rocky riverside setting (despite the forecast, I didn't need to open my fishing umbrella today) and the white noise; that deep undercurrent.

I wouldn't get that if I was interpreting this same scene from a photograph; I like the experience of drinking in a dose of wilderness.

Parkin Clough

I've followed this rocky path up Parkin Clough, the gulley running up from Yorkshire Bridge to Win Hill. There are mosses and ferns down by the little stream, oaks and holly on the steep sides of the clough and larch plantations with a few pines on the hillside on either side.

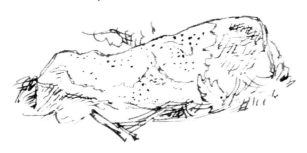

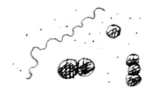

This small rock, a piece of gritty sandstone nearly one foot long, has lichen on it which has a very pale greenish-grey tinge, peppered with black dots.

Through a hand lens the sporangia of the lichen look like burnt breadcakes on old mortar. Each black sporangium is a millimetre or two across.

gold
green
moss

white fungal
growth

Larch
needles

Wiry
grass

Oak leaves

North

Bracken frond

This stump, which was probably a larch, was about 35 years old when felled. The widest growth rings are on its north side, away from the gulley and up-slope.
Did it grow like this to buttress itself against the slope?

MORE
GROWTH

EQUAL
GROWTH

If it did grow equally on both sides the tree would grow at right angles to the slope, instead of truly vertically.

The cells are somehow aware of gravity as they grow and they coordinate their growth: geotropism, negative geotropism (i.e. away from the Earth).

ears on
oak leaf
not proof positive that
it's common oak but
not pure sessile?

An April morning: billowing towers of Cumulus are stacked up over the Peak District. There's a hail storm every hour with cold breezes.

At least the rain & hail have given me a subject; this is one of the drainage gullys channelling the run-off from the hillside plantation under the track at the edge of the reservoir.

The damp, shady habitat encourages a lush growth of liverworts, mosses and ferns.

Sporangia brown

stem pale green

underside of lobe green with fine brown hairs along mid-ribs. ×1.25

Lobes about 1 cm across

Lobes olive green, lighter at edges

Liverwort

The rosettes of golden saxifrage, 4 inches (10cm) tall, grow on the rocks on the shady side of the gully.

Pale yellow-green flowers have 4 petal-like sepals & 8 yellow stamens

(although the flowers are so tiny that even with a hand lens I counted only 6)

41

42

I had to give up on this bamboo pen drawing of an old wild cherry when I was lashed by hail and it was too windy, on an exposed stretch of the waterside track, to put up the fishing umbrella. The following afternoon, when I returned to finish the drawing, it was still cool but with about 5 layers on, and a fingerless glove on my right hand, I could cope with that.

Sandstone from the track-side. I don't use pencil much because, especially with softer grades like this 6B, it soon smudges as I carry my sketchbook around.

6B

Using small screw-top sample jars that I bought at Boots' Pharmacy, I've tried mixing four washes of Chinese ink to give me an evenly spaced range of tones on location.

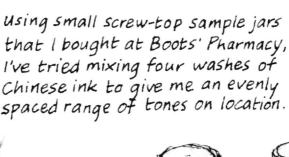

Squirrel-nibbled cone : hard F grade pencil & wash.

43

Wood Sorrel

on bank by track
through plantation
near Parkin Clough,
Win Hill
27th march

visited by
small black
hoverflies

white flowers
with lilac-grey
veins & greenish
yellow
centres

Most of the Bright green
clover-like leaves were
folded back like these.

Greater spotted
woodpecker
hides on other
side of tree

Flexible body

smaller
rove

Flattened-
shaped brown
rove beetle in
leaf/larch litter

Fern unfurling: broad
buckler fern has
brown streaks on
its stem scales, so
I'm guessing that
this is the similar-
looking male fern

Rove beetles
have short wing
cases so they
look as if they're
wearing short
jackets as they
explore the leaf
litter. They're
probably predators.

3.5cm tall
Brown/Black scales at base.
Coppery (no streaks) above

Brown wing
cases
waving
antennae
8mm

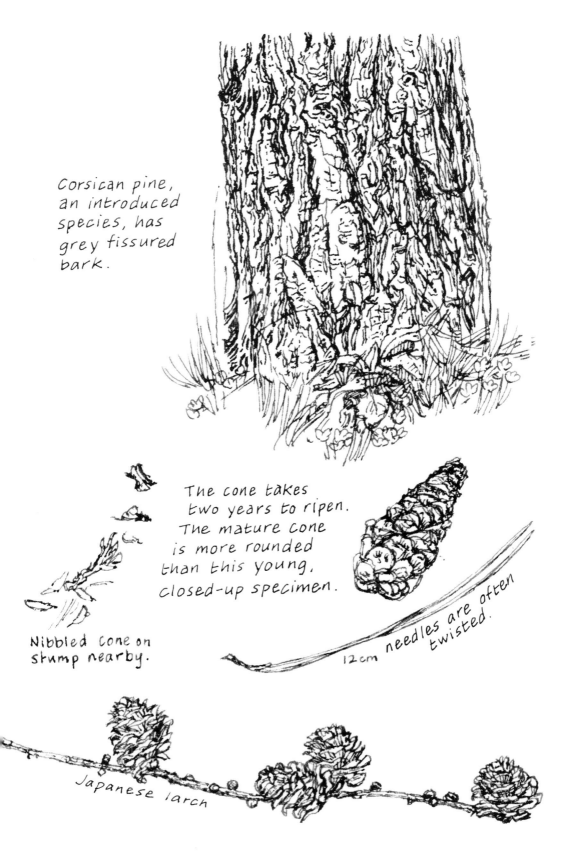

Corsican pine, an introduced species, has grey fissured bark.

The cone takes two years to ripen. The mature cone is more rounded than this young, closed-up specimen.

Nibbled cone on stump nearby.

12cm needles are often twisted.

Japanese larch

Fairholmes

The Derwent Valley wasn't
always dominated by conifers.
Looking across the top end
of Ladybower reservoir
from Fairholmes visitor
centre gives some impression
of what it was like here
before the valley was
flooded in the 1940s.

'People come up to me and say
isn't it beautiful around here,'
said local man Morris Cottrill
in a BBC film about the
sunken villages of Ladybower*
'But it's nothing to what it was.
It's all man-made now.'

My grandfather had some fishing
on the Derwent and my mum remembers the
Cottrill's farm from before the war. She remembers
playing in hay meadows on the hillside which have
long since been flooded.

washing
routine

I find the water
gives the place a
sense of peace and
this view reminds me
of the Lake District,
despite the twin
concrete aqueduct
pipes running across
the reservoir nearby.

* Inside Out-
BBC East Midlands
September 2003.

well, it would be peaceful
if it wasn't for the honking
of that Canada goose and
the ducks that gather
when you take out
your sandwiches!

47

This large beech is marked on old maps next to Fairholmes farm which stood here for some 500 years. There are still a few traces of the buildings which were demolished to make way for Ladybower reservoir.

In a photograph of Fairholmes farm taken in the 1920s there's a beech hedge running down the slope. You can still see the line of this hedge but it now runs down into the water and the beeches are now fully grown.
But they're only a quarter of the size in girth of this old tree.
It may be a pollard.

Pollarding is a method of cutting back the branches of a tree to provide a harvest of poles. New branches sprout again up out of the reach of grazing animals.

Lopped boughs of this tree have been cut into logs.

Derwent
dam, 1916

It took two years for Ladybower to fill (1943-45).
I hadn't realised that its 6,300 million gallons
aren't used for water supply: Ladybower is
there to provide compensation water to the
River Derwent, allowing the whole of the output
from Howden and Derwent to be used for
water supply.

While the two earlier dams were built in stone,
Ladybower is a rockfill embankment. It was
refurbished (1998-2000) with a 10 metre
thick rockfill layer on the downstream
slope of the dam. The rock was quarried
from Win Hill; quarrying operations were
suspended during the period that a pair of
goshawks were nesting.

Howden dam,
1901

Carl Wark
HILL FORT
9ᵗʰ May
drawn from near
Fiddler's Elbow,
Higger Tor,
looking south-east

Two or three thousand years ago, the moors must have looked very much as they do this morning.

The sun burns through the mist and drawing becomes so much easier. One morning four weeks ago the hills were covered with snow, but today I can settle down to draw in comfort on the moors above Hathersage with ravens, merlin and of course frolicsome lambs for company. Bliss!

There's a hollow with a small circular pool of water in this rock on the east end of Carl Wark. When I arrived a meadow pipit flew up out of it; perhaps it was using it as a bird bath or taking some of the aphids and black flies trapped there.

A wren perched on the edge of the rock, overlooking the valley, puffed out its chest and started to sing. The fort itself was probably a way of marking territory: Higger Tor overlooking Carl Wark in the background (left, top) looks like a more defensible position.

53

Rocks are scattered in a chunky necklace around the gritstone tor of Carl Wark. It reminds me of a kopje — a rocky redoubt favoured by leopards — on the African veld. There is a theory that the deep weathering that exploited those joints and bedding plains to produce the massive blocks dates from a time before the last ice age when Britain experienced tropical conditions, 22 to two million years ago, in the late Tertiary.

Nasal Chwey! Chwey! chup-chup-chup-chup-chup as it comes down

Meadow pipit

pursued by little bird - pipit?

Bright descending cascade of song then it parachutes down to a tuft amongst the dry bracken.

Swept-back wings. 1pm flies up from Carl Wark then dips to tops of conifers in plantation.

Merlin

12.30pm

Little mid to light brown falcon. Bit smaller than kestrel. Slowish flight 10ft above heather turning up the valley.

54

Rampart guards
most accessible
end of Carl Wark

I shouldn't be surprised, but it's obvious that, by
sitting here at the edge of this moorland gully
for an hour or so, I'm seeing more birds and insects
than I would if I was striding along over the hills.

1.05pm
what I take to be a raven,
apparently on its own, lands
on the end of the old massive
wall then flies off along
Crag & out over valley.

a single magpie
has a favoured
perch on a rock
overlooking the
valley.

1.10pm 3 ants carrying off 3 small crumbs from
my picnic through the moor grass & sheep droppings 55

The Rampart

Using my walking pole as a rough measure I got the length of this wall as 21 metres (69 ft), and the maximum height as a little under 3m (10 ft). The wall is backed by an earth bank. Many of the blocks are a metre or more long.

Gritstone rocks near the centre of the plateau. The one on the right (with the meadow pipit sitting on it) is 2.5m (8ft) high.

I spotted this shattered chunk of millstone grit by the rock on the left.

Those striations: could this be some kind of Iron Age quern stone?

Or were the scratches made when the rock got dragged along in an ice age glacier?

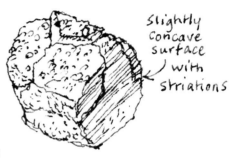

Slightly concave surface with striations

Quartz grain

Rusty crust

They're slickensides, Gaynor Boon, a geologist at Sheffield Museums tells me:

'The surface shows typical pressure effects and polish--ing in one direction with the coarseness equivalent to the grain size in the gritstone.'

Slickensides occur when rocks grind against each other during movement along a fault.

Higger Tor,

above Hathersage. 434 metres
these boulders are usually popular
with mini-bus groups of young
climbers. Not today though, perhaps
because of the strong breeze from
the south west. Apart from the
sound of the wind, the distant
cacophony of a passing school
group just adds to the wildness -
like the busy clamour of a sea-bird cliff.

Packhorse bridge
over Burbage Brook,
below Carl Wark

Stanage Edge

BEAIRRR BAIIR'

worried
bleat
from a
lamb

No wool on neck gives
this ewe a scrawny
look.

Ewe's
tail

Rook

I think this ewe
is looking for a
lost lamb. Wish
I could tell her
that I think it
went off with
a little group in
the other direction.

Each ewe that passed stopped for a
scratch. As this is a picnic bench for
wheelchair users, they were able to get
right inside to give their backs a rub.

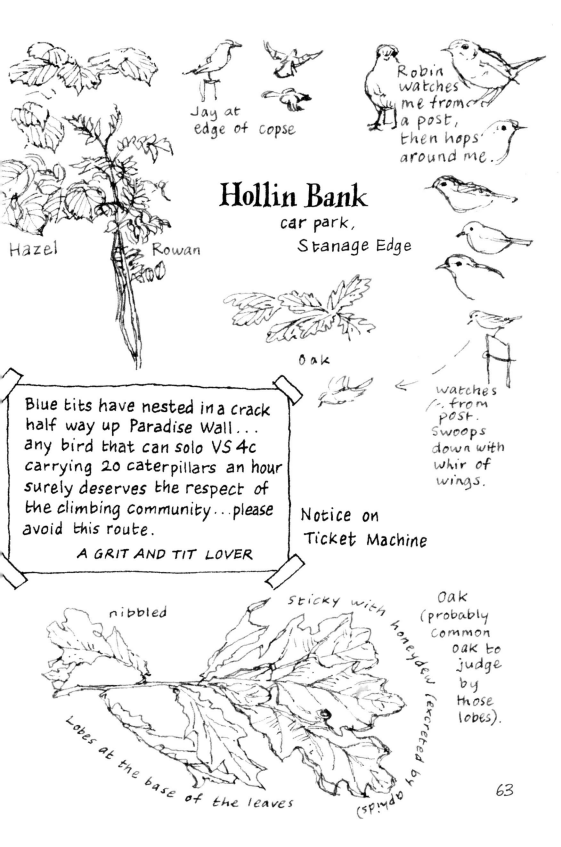

Jay at edge of copse

Hazel   Rowan

Hollin Bank

car park,
Stanage Edge

Robin watches me from a post, then hops around me.

Oak

watches from post. Swoops down with whir of wings.

Blue tits have nested in a crack half way up Paradise Wall... any bird that can solo VS 4c carrying 20 caterpillars an hour surely deserves the respect of the climbing community...please avoid this route.

A GRIT AND TIT LOVER

Notice on Ticket Machine

nibbled

sticky with honeydew (excreted by aphids)

Oak (probably common oak to judge by those lobes).

Lobes at the base of the leaves

63

64

Pheasant grockling, woodpecker drumming, cuckoo calling, lamb bleating, curlews bubbling. Hoot of a train going from the middle of Sheffield to the middle of Manchester.

4.30pm, 25°C, 10th May

A wild cherry is in blossom at the corner of the hedge line, alongside birch and rowan (not yet in blossom). Tormentil and bracken grow on this rough grassy slope by a steep stone stile. That's the spire of Hathersage church in the distance.

I spotted this perfect little valley while taking the back road between Higger Tor and Ladybower along the foot of Stanage Edge. This, the valley of the Hood Brook, and the steeper more densely wooded Hurst Clough are tucked away to the north of the Hathersage/Bamford road.

Cottages at Hathersage from a table outside Colemans Deli (we went for olives, hummus & pitta bread)

Hope,
St Peter's churchyard

Cold but sunny: it seems so strange to be sitting out _enjoying_ drawing rather than just surviving; bracing myself against the cold, wind & hail.

I didn't need the umbrella even once.

I used my Parker Reflex fountain pen to draw the carvings on this 1,000 year old Saxon cross as I felt that I needed something more controllable than bamboo pen today.

These patterns remind me of diagrams of the inside of an atom or of solar systems with planetary & cometary orbits.

Worlds within worlds.

I couldn't resist including these two characters. Whoever carved them had fun. They probably date from the 1400s when the Parish of Hope was one of the largest in England, taking in much of the Royal Hunting Forest centred on the Peak.

Lesser celandine, a relative of the buttercup, is in flower in the churchyard.

St Peter in his niche on the porch.

67

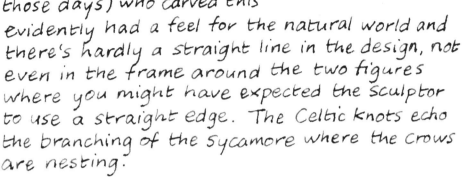

The artist (not that there was such a career as 'artist' in those days) who carved this evidently had a feel for the natural world and there's hardly a straight line in the design, not even in the frame around the two figures where you might have expected the sculptor to use a straight edge. The Celtic knots echo the branching of the sycamore where the crows are nesting.

Two jackdaws, stashing twigs in a niche over the porch, behind the bearded figure of St Peter who is holding the keys of heaven, remind me of the two ravens who in Viking myth kept flying back to Odin to keep him abreast of goings on in the world of men.

Pierced by his own spear, Odin, sometimes known as All-father, hung on the world tree for nine days to learn the secret of the runes. I wonder if this was the reason that this cross - in Anglian style but with a Viking influence - was carved to resemble a tree: it might represent a time of change in the spiritual life of the Hope Valley.

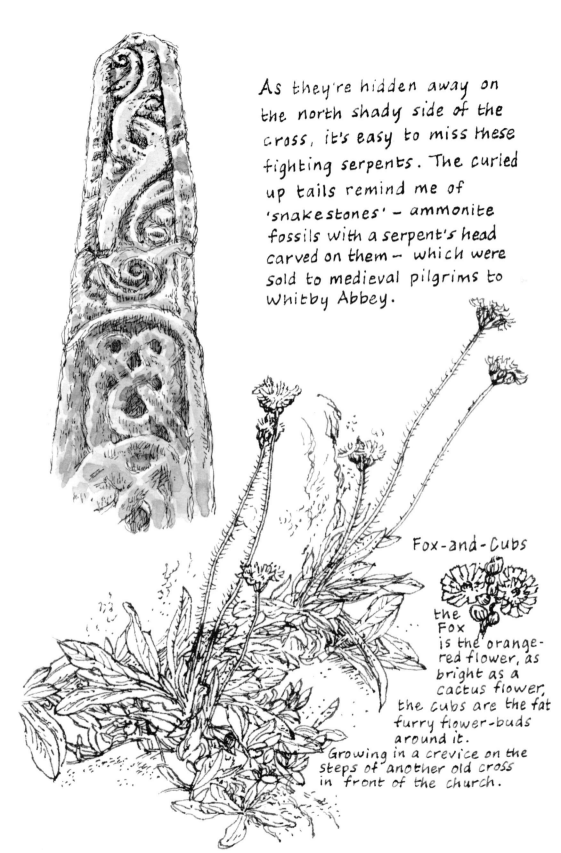

As they're hidden away on the north shady side of the cross, it's easy to miss these fighting serpents. The curled up tails remind me of 'snakestones' – ammonite fossils with a serpent's head carved on them – which were sold to medieval pilgrims to Whitby Abbey.

Fox-and-Cubs

the Fox is the orange-red flower, as bright as a cactus flower, the cubs are the fat furry flower-buds around it.
Growing in a crevice on the steps of another old cross in front of the church.

Castleton

So many walkers miss the entrance to Cave Dale,
realise their mistake then double back. This is
it: right here — up the yard between Dale Cottage
and Cavedale Cottage. It must be the most
cunningly concealed dale in the country.

Cat with
Freisian Cow
markings

Cave Dale

As I approach the gate at the end of the yard it's so narrow that I can easily stretch out my hands and touch both rock-faces.

On a shady ledge Maidenhair Spleenwort, so called because its spleen-shaped leaves resemble those of the maidenhair fern, grows to 3 or 4 inches (10 cm). 'Wort' in a plant name implied that it had a medicinal value and, according to the doctrine of signatures, if it resembled a spleen it should be effective in treating infirmities of the spleen. Culpeper (1653) also suggests it for bladder stones, jaundice and hiccups.

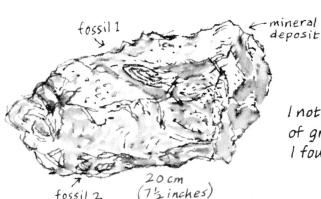

fossil 1 ← mineral deposit

↗ fossil 2

20 cm
(7½ inches)

Looking at Limestone

I noticed a fossil in this piece of greyish limestone which I found near the castle.

Flat shell

It was the pattern of concentric rings on this shell which stood out. It's a brachiopod and I'm pretty sure this is Echinoconchus punctatus, a species which is found here around Castleton. Brachiopods are sometimes known as lamp shells because some species resemble Roman oil lamps; the hole for the wick was for a stalk which attached them to the sea bed.

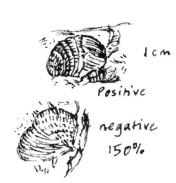

1 cm

Positive

negative

150%

Once I looked more closely at the rock, I spotted these fingernail-sized shells of another brachiopod, Antiquatonia hindi (again I'm 99% sure that's the species, but I'm no expert). There's a positive and a negative mould of the shells; the lower one is indented into the rock.

Despite appearances, brachiopods aren't related to molluscs such as clams & cockles.

I'm no expert at identifying minerals either but I know a test for hardness helps.

'The mineral is interesting.' said a geologist friend, 'If you could scratch it with a fingernail then it was probably gypsum not calcite which is odd. But I have found some strange minerals at Castleton - it is famous for them.'

You can scratch calcite with a penknife.

Lustrous, white opaque can scratch with finger nail

Limestone crag near
the castle, Cave Dale.
Jackdaws nesting in
some of the cavities.

74

The top end
of Cave Dale.

rubbing
itself on a
rock.

scratching in a
little cave

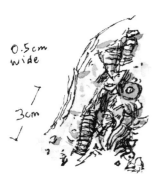

0.5cm wide

3cm

These fossil fragments of crinoid (sea lily), resembling pieces of pasta, were in a loose block which, appropriately, I found up near the top of the dale; when Cave Dale was a tropical reef, some 320 million years ago, crinoids lived at the top of the reef. An animal, designed like a starfish on a stem, the crinoid spread its arms to catch food fragments wafting up on currents from the depths below.

The snails at the bottom of the dale are stripy brown-lipped snails. These plain pale ochre snails from a rocky platform near the top end of the dale look like a colour variation of the same species.

Matriach of the Dale

12 sheep

Drawing sheep is so soothing. There isn't really a 'wrong' pose to draw them in. If I don't like one pose, there'll be another along in a minute. This little flock of a dozen never did anything more striking than occasionally scratch against a rock, meet in the odd head-to-head over a tuft of grass or panic slightly on realising that their companions had ambled off along the slope.

Peveril Castle

My granddad Maurice Swift, a
cabinet maker and funeral director
from Sheffield, bought this oil
painting of the castle from Castleton
artist Ernest Bowler in the 1920s.
We inherited the picture from
granddad in the 1960s so I've known
the scene for 40 years but never
visited Cave Dale until now.
I always wondered if Bowler had
romanticized the situation — no;
that's pretty much the way it is.

'When I was a boy,' a dog walker
tells me, 'we found a cave up
there and we could climb out in
the castle grounds but they've
blocked it up with concrete now.
I know that when you're young
you imagine things, but I'm sure
that one part of it was made
up with old stonework.'

Toasted teacakes & a pot of tea in the
Stables Tearoom at the Old Nag's Head   79

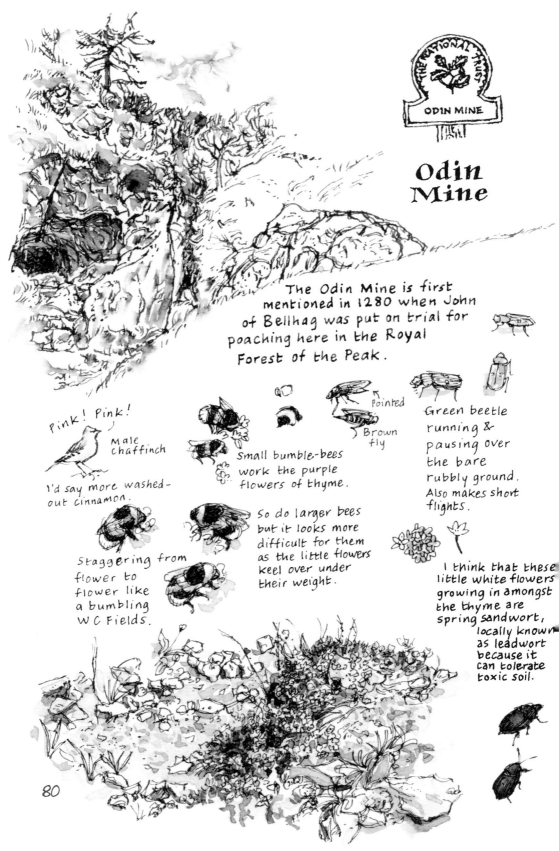

Odin Mine

ODIN MINE

The Odin Mine is first mentioned in 1280 when John of Bellhag was put on trial for poaching here in the Royal Forest of the Peak.

Pink! Pink!

Male chaffinch

I'd say more washed-out cinnamon.

Small bumble-bees work the purple flowers of thyme.

Pointed

Brown fly

Green beetle running & pausing over the bare rubbly ground. Also makes short flights.

Staggering from flower to flower like a bumbling W C Fields.

So do larger bees but it looks more difficult for them as the little flowers keel over under their weight.

I think that these little white flowers growing in amongst the thyme are spring sandwort, locally known as leadwort because it can tolerate toxic soil.

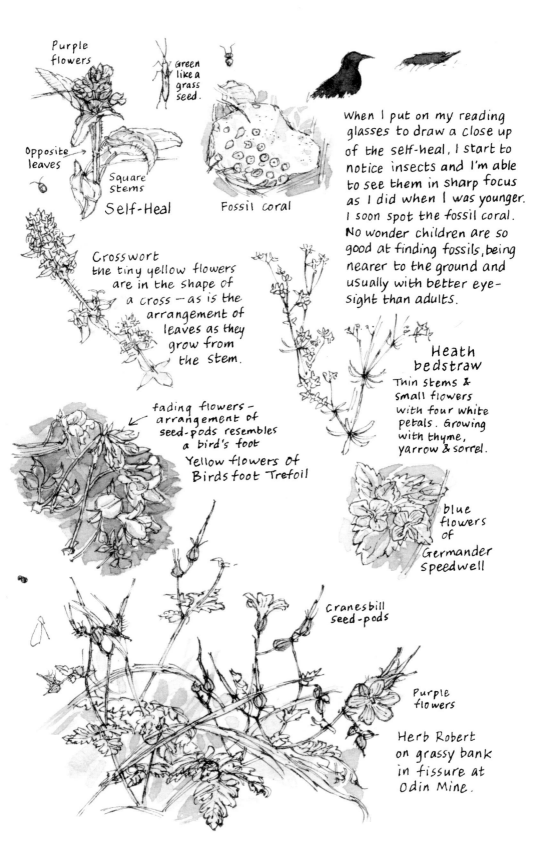

Purple flowers

Green like a grass seed.

Opposite leaves

Square stems

Self-Heal

Fossil coral

When I put on my reading glasses to draw a close up of the self-heal, I start to notice insects and I'm able to see them in sharp focus as I did when I was younger. I soon spot the fossil coral. No wonder children are so good at finding fossils, being nearer to the ground and usually with better eye-sight than adults.

Crosswort
the tiny yellow flowers are in the shape of a cross — as is the arrangement of leaves as they grow from the stem.

Heath bedstraw
Thin stems & small flowers with four white petals. Growing with thyme, yarrow & sorrel.

fading flowers – arrangement of seed-pods resembles a bird's foot
Yellow flowers of Birds foot Trefoil

blue flowers of Germander speedwell

Cranesbill seed-pods

Purple flowers

Herb Robert on grassy bank in fissure at Odin Mine.

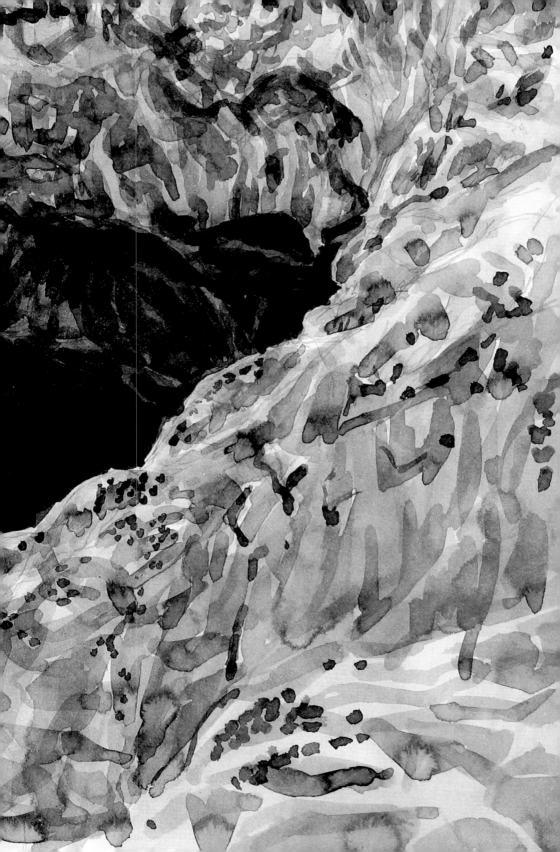

Lapis lazuli damselfly

Yellow & black hunting wasp 3 cm long on rushes.

Loud high-pitched dispute by waterside (also croaks) then this big black sausage of a creature darts out from the undergrowth. Water shrew? Water voles are seen here.

faded magenta flowers

24 cm 10 inches tall

Orchid, probably a marsh orchid, Dactylorhiza sp.

growing amongst rushes & horsetails by pond.

Palmate Newt

Palmate has large feet.

The water is clear enough for me to see the newts on the stony bed of the pond.

The male, which has a ribbon-like tail is following a female (round tail).

There are two different water plants here: the oval leaves and the rat's tail flower spike (top left) belong to a pondweed but the five-petalled white flowers are a kind of water-crowfoot, which has submerged leaves.

Roadside Pond

near the foot of the
landslip below Mam Tor

Whitethroat

Also sings
in short
gliding
flights.

Little torrents
of scratchy song
sometimes from
post, branch or
top of bracken.

2 or 3
Swallows appear & start
dipping down at
the pond

PLIP!

bathing?
drinking?
catching insects?

3.45 pm

To judge by the splash they
make this is more than just
grabbing a drink. My guess
is that they're bathing.

male
newt
swimming
down into
the pond.

Although there
are plenty of
insects for them
to catch.

Hundreds of little black flies
dance just above the water surface
while other perch on grasses at
the water's edge.

A pond skater
is on the look
out for any insect trapped
on the surface film.

The Shivering Mountain

Like Carl Wark, Mam Tor was occupied as a hill fort.

Radiocarbon dating indicates that there has been movement on the Mam Tor landslip over the last 3,000 years. The shales on the slopes of the hill can become particularly unstable when a dry summer is followed by a wet winter, as happened in 1976-77.

The unwise decision to build a road across the landslip was made 200 years ago; in 1802 the Manchester and Sheffield Turnpike Company opened the route to offer an alternative to the steep gradients of Winnats Pass.

The landslip now extends 920 metres (over half a mile) into the valley and has an average gradient of 1 in 5. The small pond that I've been drawing lies near the toe of the landslip.

Manchester University is monitoring movement and weather conditions as part of a long term study.

The figures that I've quoted above are given by Derbyshire County Council Environmental Services.

I didn't realise that the name Mam Tor means just what you might think it means: the Mother Hill. That seems appropriate; the way it perches at the top of the dale, like a mother hen.

I find it hard to believe that when I came drawing in the Peak District in the spring of 1979, this was still an A road, the A625 between Sheffield and Manchester, although it was already down to one lane and it was abandoned altogether later that year.

This morning the only traffic — apart from hikers & school groups — is a single cyclist but he has to be doggedly determined to make it to the top.

Kinderscout Moors

To Mam Tor

Hollins Cross

The View from Treak Cliff

Small geranium in shady crevice in limestone.

this white-flowered relative of stitchwort seems to survive being nibbled by spreading low on the turf

After I've drawn this panorama from the ridge above Treak Cliff cavern I decide to have my sandwiches before drawing this spear thistle. As I'm eating them, along comes this hummingbird hawkmoth, zooming over to the flower just three feet from me and using its long thin tongue to probe the individual florets. There's a stiffish breeze but by humming those wings (though I couldn't hear a buzz) it was able to keep perfectly in position as it performed the operation with precision. It's a migrant species but it's possible that some now over-winter here. It's the most un-mothlike of moths.

90

Limestone ridge

• Do I give up on bamboo pen?! It's so uncontrollable - but I like the effect.

Lose Hill

When I first walked up Lose Hill last autumn I found myself climbing into cloud. It reminded me of climbing up to the cloud base from Manchester airport. A stone causeway like an Inca trail took me to the viewpoint, lost in the mist, at the summit. The cloud had cleared by the time I'd walked along the ridge to Mam Tor but it is so exposed up there that as I came down the steps on the other side the wind blew me over.

PERCHING ON A SHELTERED ROCK OVER-LOOKING THE NETTLE PATCH. WINGS OPENED TO THE NOON-DAY SUN.

As I draw the view from the ridge these sheep take a break nearby on the turf amongst the spear thistles. In the shelter of the limestone outcrop (which 320 million years ago formed the top of a reef) there's a bed of nettles. Two small tortoiseshell butterflies chase around above the nettle-tops: nettles are the food plant of their caterpillars.

12mm Reddish brown

notch between wing cases and thorax. The click beetle can trigger this to spring itself over if it finds itself on its back.

darker brown click beetle

I have a distinct feeling
of vertigo as I perch on
a windswept precipice
overlooking Winnats Pass.

It's like being up in the
gods in a theatre.

Tchucu! (LIKE
Tchuk! PEBBLE
CLACK)
Tchuck!

Ring Ousel

Exactly like a blackbird –
perhaps a bit brownish – but
didn't sound anything like a
blackbird as it flew up the
slope. Later flew across pass
to rocks on other side.

This milestone still stands by the abandoned stretch of the A625 on the Mam Tor landslip.

The footpath (top right) takes you up out of the Hope Valley via Hollins Cross, a ridge-top meeting of ways, over into the Vale of Edale.

SHEFFIELD
17 MILES
HATHERSAGE
7 MILES

CHAPEL EN LE
FRITH
5 MILES
SPARROWPIT.

93

Jacob's Ladder

WHINCHAT

Tchat
Chat
Chat
Chat

Buffish
Alarmed
scolding

also
grouse &
sheep.

If you keep on walking beyond Barber Booth, at the top end of the Vale of Edale, you'll arrive at this Peak District stairway to heaven; a rugged causeway that takes you up onto the moors around Kinderscout.

Three large black birds perch on the hand-rail at the top, chatting and flapping about rather acrobatically. They are, I guess, ravens, not crows; we're on the edge of their moorland domain.

The whinchat, another bird of open country, is sometimes known as the 'furze-chat' because of its habit of perching on top of gorse bushes.

The moors are closed this evening because of the summer fire risk but rights of way are still open and a solitary hiker sets off up the Ladder, from bridge to brink in 3½ minutes.

Paul Klee described drawing as going for a walk with a line. When I'm drawing a mossy rock or a gnarled old tree trunk, I find myself exploring its surface — looking at its grain, its facets and crevices — as if I was an ant crawling about on it. My hand follows my eye while the pen traces the journey, as if the rock is a landscape in itself.

It's like that when I'm walking too; I want to stride along and see how the landscape unfolds before me, to absorb its shapes, its character and its texture. I like to drift. Think things through. Or not even to think really; just go into free-fall and lose myself in the landscape (which sometimes caused a few comments in the days when I used to lead a walks group, but I always brought them back in time).

So drawing and walking are essentially the same for me: a way of seeing, an exploration; a journey to the surface of the earth.

18ᵗʰ century guide post (c.1709) found in 2000 placed in churchyar by Hope Historica Society 2003

3.M. Darwent Roc Three-sided